Old Sil[…]onby

Tr[…]

In 1150 the Cistercian Order selected the remote marshes of Holm Cultrum to build their abbey. Sea dykes were built reclaiming land and creating prosperous farms, run by 140 monks and 600 lay brothers, generating enough wealth for the Abbey to surpass Carlisle Cathedral in size. The Scots attacked in 1216 and again in 1318 when Robert the Bruce sacked the Abbey, until bought off with £200 a year 'protection money'. When Henry VIII dissolved Holm Cultrum in 1536 the abbey had only 25 monks. Petitioned by the local people, the nave was saved as a parish church but was too large to maintain. In 1724 the aisles were removed and the east end brought forward, resulting in the church we see in this photograph. In recent years Holm Cultrum was an arts centre, until an arson attack in 2006 destroyed the roof and many holy relics.

Heavy seas crash into the sea defences at Skinburness, but it was not always so well protected. In 1300 it was an expanding market town, raising 100 marks a year in tax for the Crown, and able to provision Edward I's Scottish invasion fleet of 58 ships and 1099 men, when disaster struck. In 1302 it was washed away when the sea dyke gave way. Many of the inhabitants settled at Newton Arlosh, building a new village, and the church intended for Skinburness, in 1303.

First published in the United Kingdom, 2007,
by Stenlake Publishing Ltd.
www.stenlake.co.uk
ISBN 9781840334197

Acknowledgements

For help with compiling this book the author would like to thank: Captain Chris Puxley, Fausto & Christine Previtali of The Golf Hotel, Ashley Kendall, Dennis Perriam, Ralph Pickering, Nancy Sowerby, Irene Bell, Malcolm MacDonald, Major A J R Harrison, Robert Grieves and the late Nellie Twentyman.

Picture Acknowledgements

Golf Hotel: P2, P6, P7, P9, P10, P12, P15, P25, P26, P28, P29, P31, P33.

Ashley Kendall: P13, P14, P19, P21, P30, P34, P35, P42

Further Reading

The books listed below were used by the author during his research. None are available from Stenlake Publishing Ltd; please contact your local bookshop or reference library.

Brian Blake, *The Solway Firth*, pub. The Regional Books, 1955.
John Britton, *Beauties of England & Wales*, printed by J Harris, London, 1802.
William Hutchinson, *The History of the County of Cumberland*, printed by F Jollie, 1794.
George Neilson, *Annals of the Solway*, pub. 1896, reprinted Michael Moon, 1974.
John Pearson and Peter Cusack, *Golf at Silloth*, pub. Silloth Golf Club, 2002.
Mary Scott-Parker, *Silloth*, pub. Bookcase, 1998.
Stephen White, *Solway Steam*, pub. Carel Press, 1984.

INTRODUCTION

The Solway coast is Cumbria's best kept secret, visitors to the nearby Lake District, not knowing this Area of Outstanding Natural Beauty. It is dominated by the sea, marshes, creeks and sandy shores, with charming settlements that once rang to the tramp of legionnaire's feet and the hooves of Reiver's horses. A place of legend - a place of history.

Hugging the coast road south of Newton Arlosh, beside the river Waver, lies the small residential village of Abbeytown, whose abbey once dominated the English Solway. Petitioned by the Cistercian Abbey at Melrose, King David of Scotland granted land at Holm Cultrum for an abbey, completed in 1192, but later taken over by Henry ll of England.

Wearing distinctive white woollen habits, the Cistercian order rejected the luxurious lifestyle of their Benedictine brothers, preferring to devote their lives to worship and work. The years passed, and the abbey estates increased, with vast sheep-walks created on reclaimed land, and granges or home farms established as far south as Mawbray. Holm Cultrum wool was exported to Flanders and envious eyes were cast on the abbey's wealth. Edward l held Court here, whilst Scottish raiders sacked, burned and looted it.

The years of anarchy took their toll and when Henry VIII dissolved the abbey in 1536 only a handful of monks remained. Most of the Abbey building was dismantled, the stone taken to build local houses, but part of it was saved as a parish church, and refuge from the Scots. In 2006 the abbey was damaged by fire, and a fund was set up by the vicar, David Tembey, and his parishioners to restore the abbey to its former glory.

North west of Abbeytown lies the former port and market town of Skinburness. On its narrow peninsula, the 13th century port was used by Holm Cultrum to export wool, salted fish and salt to Ireland and Scotland. Favouring it as a naval base, Edward l made Skinburness a free borough, *with all liberties and free customs forever ... a weekly market on Thursday and a fair every year.* Permission had just been granted to build a parish church when, in 1302, the sea dyke was breached and as recorded in the Parliamentary Roles "with the breaking in of the ocean, the town was laid to waste". Skinburness remains a place of mystery, with the "Long House" (now terraced houses), featured in Walter Scott's novel *Redgauntlet*, once the haunt of smugglers, and Grune Point reputedly where Sir Gawain of King Arthur's Round Table fought the Green Knight.

In 1847 neighbouring Silloth was ridiculed as a rabbit warren by Henry Jacob secretary of the Maryport and Carlisle Railway Company, a mere hamlet with surrounding farmhouses, which, within a few years was transformed into an elegant seaside resort. Its development is a tale of Victorian rashness, speculation and entrepreneurial enterprise, on a grand scale. With the failure of the Carlisle Canal, the City of Carlisle wished to remain independent from the West Cumberland ports, and needed a deep water dock. Silloth Bay was selected and a railway line run from Drumburgh junction to the 'rabbit warren'. Work on Silloth port began, but it soon became apparent that established railways were taking freight traffic from Silloth. Undeterred the directors of the Carlisle and Silloth Bay Railway speculated further, purchased the remainder of Blitterlees Common beside the dock and built the Victorian resort of Silloth we know today.

Silloth became the county's premier seaside resort and was short-listed as a possibility for King George V convalescence in 1929. Guidebooks extolled it's attractions - the invigorating air, temperate climate, airy streets, boat trips, entertainments, promenade, beach - and tourists flocked in, until the 1960s when the availability of cheap foreign package holidays changed the fortunes of all British seaside resorts. Hordes of summer visitors no longer descend from the railway station, and Silloth is now a serene and unspoiled gem

If Silloth is the new town, Allonby represents the old. Hutchinson's History of the County of Cumberland of 1794 describes Allonby as, *a small neat, pleasant market town; and a bathing place of considerable resort*, and the *Beauties of England and Wales* by John Britton of 1802 says Allonby was, *a neat well-built town resorted to in the summer season.* Once a Quaker settlement, with its wealth founded on agriculture and intermittent fishing. Horse racing was held on the sands, and a sea water baths, with impressive Ionic columns, opened in 1835, whilst Charles Dickens chose Allonby for an episode in his book, *The Lazy Tour of Two Idle Apprentices*, being *the most delicious piece of sea coast to be found within the limits of England, Ireland, Scotland, Wales, the Isle of Man and the Channel Islands all summed up together.* Dickens' impression, when he arrived in Allonby village was not quite so complimentary, although he did approve of the sunsets.

But Allonby, unlike Silloth, seemed reluctant to develop fully. Half hearted attempts were made to bring the railway and build a landing stage, but failed, and when the baths closed in 1900, Allonby's dream of becoming a fashionable resort vanished. Today, Allonby has retained its character, with its groups of brightly painted houses on either side of The Beck, and its hidden cobbled lanes and curious corners, it is still the quaint village beside Alan's Bay.

Abbeytown village from the Wigton road in 1908. On the left is John Little's grocer shop, and stockist of Carr & Co of Silloth's flour. The shop is now a private house, whilst the cottage to its right has had a second storey added. The remaining properties on this side have been demolished to allow road widening. On the right is Chatworth Square and the Joiners Arms, landlord John Park. The hedge further to the right, later replaced with railings, bounds Abbeytown School playground.

Abbeytown looking towards the crossroads around 1905, with the bay fronted Waver Terrace on the left, and John Little's shop in the centre distance. On the right is Abbeytown School, built in 1853 for £450. It was endowed with scholarships, by John Longcake of Pelutho House, of £25 a year to the best boy or girl, and £20 to the most deserving boy over a three year period. In 1879 the school was examined by the Rev H M Todd who found Bible knowledge, catechism and repetition of the scholars satisfactory, and the staff and pupils passed the inspection with great credit.

Early 19th century holidaymakers made the difficult journey to the Skinburness Inn via the ferry from Annan, and in an 1833 edition of the *Carlisle Journal*, The Skinburness Inn thanks; ... *The English and Scottish Nobility, Gentry and Public for the many favours conveyed upon the hotel*. It was described as; ... *delightful and convenient* ... and ... *adapted for invalids and those who seek only recreation*. The facilities included; ... *hot baths and private sitting rooms*, whilst, *the sands are not as bad as frequently reported*. The development of Silloth brought a coach road to Skinburness, and with more tourists the inn was rebuilt in the 1880s by Edwin Hodge Banks (1847-1917) of Highmoor, Wigton to a design by the architect Charles John Ferguson (1840-1904) as the Skinburness Hydro and Hotel, as shown in this 1909 photograph.

A Jowett 'long four tourer', introduced in 1926 by the Jowett Company of Bradford (closed 1954), parked on the marsh road. On the left is Midtown Farm beside Pond Cottage and the village pond, now drained. Beyond the cottage is the Skinburness Hotel, with Whiteways Farm on the right by the sloping sea dyke. Skinburness Marsh is divided into "Stints" or portions of pasture and let for grazing. During the Second World War pill-boxes were built to guard against enemy landings, a fine example surviving at Grune Point.

Skinburness creek looking towards the village. The creek lies below the sea dyke, strengthened by the Cistercian monks of Holm Cultrum. In 1888 it became the responsibility of 'the sixteen men' of Holm Cultrum - four landowners elected each year for a period of four years - who ran the Seadyke Charity and were empowered to collect rents to maintain the dyke. Until 1995 the charity still cared for a small section of the dyke, now the responsibility of the National River Authority.

In 1857 the Liverpool architect, J W Hay, designed and built the new town of Silloth on the Victorian improved principle, with spacious, tree lined, streets on a grid pattern. At the bottom left of this grid is Station Road, then Criffel Street at the junction with Lawn Terrace on the edge of the Green. Opposite Lawn Terrace is the awning of S & H Martin, stationer and newsagent, at the junction with Eden Street, who sold this photograph as a postcard. Other streets leading off Criffel Street were also named after rivers flowing into the Solway; Wampool Street, and the end of Esk Street are in this photograph, whilst Caldew Street and Waver Street are further north.

Passengers gather on Silloth Railway Station platform as the Carlisle train arrives. The Parliamentary Bill authorising the Carlisle and Silloth Bay Railway and Dock Co to construct a line connecting the Carlisle and Port Carlisle Railway at Drumburgh Junction to Silloth Bay was passed in 1855, despite protests from Maryport, which opposed a rival dock. The line opened on 28th August 1856, with a special day's holiday in Carlisle, as nearly 3000 well-wishers caught the train to inspect the site of Silloth's intended Dock and Pier.

The MV *Noord* delivering grain to Carr's flour mill in the New Dock. Opened in 1886 by Henry Carr (1835-1904), eldest son of Carr's founder Jonathan Dodgson Carr (1806-1884), by 1905 it had grown to five storeys, and, powered by a Carel of Ghent steam engine, production increased from 16 to 30 bags per hour. However, poor quality wheat and a £90,000 overdraft, raised for the improvements, nearly bankrupted the company. The chairman, Theodore Carr (1866-1931), nephew of the founder, split the company into three and went public, with the Silloth Mill becoming Carr's Flour Mills Ltd in 1908. Today they still import Canadian wheat, providing welcome business to Silloth Docks, now owned by Associated British Ports PLC.

The paddle tug *Petrel* towing two sailing ships from Silloth New Dock into Marshall Dock in the 1900s. The Dock, named after William Marshall (1796-1872) MP for East Cumberland, opened on 3rd August 1859, and once again Carlisle's citizens were given a holiday. However, the railway company failed to anticipate the huge crowds and had to use cattle trucks to convey 17,000 spectators to Silloth to watch the steamship *Silloth*, followed by the *Wasp* and *Cumbria*, sail into the Marshall Dock.

The tug *Petrel* towing a barge of dredged mud into the Solway in 1907. Silloth's first tug, the steam driven *Arabian*, was purchased by the Silloth Bay Navigation Co. in 1863 and superceded in 1886 by the Leith built, *Solway*. It, in turn, was replaced in 1896 by the *Petrel*, powered by a two cylinder side lever engine. By 1948, the heavily worked *Petrel* was hardly seaworthy, and scrapped.

Built to protect Marshall Dock from silt and to provide a landing stage, Silloth's 1000 feet pier dates from 1857, although by the time of this 1925 photograph the end had subsided. Rounding the pier is the steamship *Yarrow*. Built in 1893 by R Napier and Sons, Glasgow, she carried livestock on the Silloth - Douglas - Dublin run. From 1929, as the *Assaroe*, she was operated by the Dublin and Silloth Steamship Co surviving a German aerial attack on 15th May 1941. She was bought in 1943 by Palgrave Murphy of Dublin to transport horses to Lisbon. On the right, the signal pole with balloon indicates there is sufficient water in the dock for the *Yarrow*.

Passengers on the pier awaiting the next steamship in, or around, 1906. It was a regular, safe, stop for steamships, but when it opened in 1857 the *Carlisle Patriot* newspaper reported that "sea captains are finding the pier far from safe". In May 1857 the *Mary Ann* of Maryport, with a cargo of slates, broke free of her moorings during a south west gale, and the alarmed captain promptly departed for Maryport without loading coals, remarking that he had never been to such a place. Only with the opening of the Marshall Dock in August 1859 could vessels berth safely during poor weather.

East Cote Lighthouse in 1919, five years after its renovation by the North British Railway Co. Erected in 1864, it complimented the pier lighthouse, one mile away, by jointly lighting the safe passage through the Silloth Channel. Originally mounted on rails, the entire lighthouse could be moved as the channel sandbanks altered, and only in 1914 was it fixed in place. In 1930 the light was automated, and in 1997 dismantled and renovated by Associated British Ports. It is represented on Silloth Junior School badge, a reminder of Silloth's Victorian heritage.

Built at Messrs Bell's shipyard at Bowness on Solway in 1840, the *Solway* Lightship assisted the safe passage of vessels to Carlisle Canal, until its closure in 1853. From 1859, until it was beached at Skinburness during a ferocious storm in 1920, it was anchored on Robin Rigg Shallows to light the channel to Marshall Dock. No longer seaworthy it was converted to a tearoom by William Ferguson of New Street, Silloth, with entry up a gangplank. When it closed in 1923, it was stripped - the deck bell sold to Silloth Golf Club - and broken up in 1929.

Silloth from the Golf Club steps, with the rear of Lawn Terrace on the left behind the rolling stock. Today the rails have gone and extensions to Carr's Flour Mill and D A Harrison's ready mixed cement silos occupy the area. In the centre can be seen the crowds on Station Road, and the spire of Christ Church on Criffel Street. Right, is the railway station, closed in 1964 and demolished in 2007.

The West Beach is Silloth's hidden gem, visitors walking the Promenade or The Green and often forgetting the beach. Those who know, however, can enjoy the sun and sea, and perhaps an ice cream or lemonade from the tea-hut. In the background is the pier, neglected and reduced to 200 feet in length after the 1959 collapse. The carefully managed marram grass stabilised the sand dunes and protected the golf course, off to the right.

The 1860 *Silloth Gazette* reminded its female readers that - *to avoid a violation of decency* - they should bathe near the town centre, leaving the gentlemen to swim at East Cote Lighthouse, and to use the bathing boxes opposite Alma Terrace. When this 1905 picture was taken, attitudes to mixed bathing had relaxed, but John Bell's Silloth Boats and Chairs Company's bathing machines were still in demand. Indeed, with the *Carlisle Journal* still writing of, *the shocking sight of men and women tumbling about in the water without a sense of decency*, the prudish could still change in a box, which was horse drawn to the water's edge.

During the summer season fisherman supplemented their income with sailings from Silloth to Grune Point, Beckfoot or Annan. Temporary landing stages were placed on the shore from the Marshall Dock to Skinburness and passengers taken by rowing boat to the fishing boats. This 1924 photograph shows the precarious procedure in operation and that enterprising fishermen were coming from further afield – the closest boat, BA442, was registered at Ballantrae in south-west Scotland.

In the 1890s Silloth's seawall consisted of large sandstone blocks set in cement but, unable to stop severe sea erosion, in 1908 a 1411 yard concrete seawall was built from North House to East Cote, and extended in 1913 to protect Ryehills Road. In 1947 storm waves washed away the wall from the Lifeboat Station to North House so a new stepped wall with promenade shown in this 1960's photograph was built. To the left and below the hill top shelter behind the promenade is Silloth Baths, owned by John Bell in 1885. Over one hundred gallons of fresh seawater were pumped into the baths with every tide. When Bell died in 1920 the Baths were offered to Holme Cultrum District Council for £1350, but the offer was declined and they were eventually converted into an amusement arcade.

The children's paddling pool and sand pit, tucked away in a clearing between the Pine Woods on The Green have changed little since this photograph was taken in the 1960s. Beyond The Green, left, is Park Terrace and, to the right, Marine Terrace on Criffel Street.

In March 1859 the *Carlisle Journal* reported that; *In Criffel Street ... an elegant row of ornamental houses with balconies on front command a fine view of the sea...whilst two large and handsome hotels, commodious and comfortable, have been built.* One of these hotels, *The Solway*, is on the right of this picture of Criffel Street. Owned by John Harding in the 1860s you could take a room with bath for 5/- per day, and a private drawing room for 10/- per week. Dog carts and carriages were provided, and the hotel even possessed its own bathing machines.

In 1886 the Carlisle architect George Dale Oliver (1851-1928) proposed that a crescent of villas be built facing the sea on Mr C Hylton Joliffe's estate, from Alma Terrace, along Skinburness Road, to East Cote. This ambitious crescent was never built and instead a variety of styled properties, as shown on this picture, were built.

Edwardian tourists, some with luggage, stream up Station Road. By the 1900's many employers permitted their workers a week's unpaid annual holiday. Silloth was a popular destination, with ten hotels and 120 lodging houses providing accommodation.

1950's day-trippers stroll along Criffel Street, past The Green, with the Solway Hotel on the right and The Balmoral Hotel at the terrace end. Opposite, is the awning of Wood's Bazaar on Wampool Street and further up, the spire of Christ Church. Built for £7700, raised by public subscription, in 1878, the Irish grey granite was transported free, as ballast, in the North British Railway Company's steamships. In the Gothic style, it has a three-storey tower and spire, with a clock added in 1878 as a memorial to the Victorian philanthropist George Moore (1806-1876) of Whitehall.

In 1908 Charles and Lillian Hawkin, eager to profit from the Edwardian fashion for medical baths, converted the Temperance Hotel on Marine Terrace into the Silloth Hydro. The baths offered included Sulphur, Seaweed, Sea-salt and, the most popular, Turkish - considered by hydro-therapists to be a virtual cure all. The Hydro's reputation grew and other treatments, including massage and chiropody, were introduced.

Eden Street from the junction with Solway Street on the right, looking down to Criffel Street. The shop on the corner is listed as Julia Greenwood's grocer and general dealer in Bulmers 1901 Directory, whilst further down the terrace is the Waverley Hotel run by Margaret and Agnes Thom. At the end of the terrace is the Solway Hotel, now the Golf Hotel, overlooking The Green.

On the left of this 1923 photograph, at 2-4 Wampool Street and 9 Criffel Street is J Wood & Co's bazaar and showroom. As an ironmonger and grocer it dates from 1860 being one of the first shops to open in modern Silloth. By the 1900s it had expanded into the adjoining premises on Criffel Street, promising in advertisements that everything was *Cheap and Good and Whatever you want, go or send to Woods*. Now a department store, you could buy virtually everything and even bank your money and no visit to Silloth was complete without calling at Woods to see the latest in Oriental china or Parisian furniture. Today the Wampool Street premises is the Blue Dolphin Cafe.

Brown's Milk Bar, a confectionery and gift shop, at 11 and 13 Station Road was only a one minute walk from the railway station, and ideally placed for thirsty travellers waiting for their train.

The North British Railway Company realised that a golf course was essential if Silloth was to prosper. The company's first course was opened east of the dock crossing The Green, but was switched in 1892 to Blitterlees Bank. Although special trains from Carlisle were run for golfers, membership of the club was poor and in the 1890s the struggling Silloth and Carlisle Clubs amalgamated. By 1902 the club had 222 members and able to built a proper clubhouse. Although the new clubhouse had gentlemen's changing facilities, a smoking room and mixed dining room, there was no changing room for the ladies, who had to use an old tennis pavillion. In 1907-08 the Carlisle club split from Silloth and in 1908 the Silloth Clubhouse was extended as per this photograph to include a ladies rest room. Today the Silloth course is a championship venue and among the top 20 courses in the UK and Ireland.

In 1858 Richard Carruthers of Eden Grove donated £250 towards, *a sea-bathing institution for the special benefit of sufferers* to convalesce after illness, and a public subscription fund was set up, with the Silloth Bay Railway & Dock Co donating land at West Silloth. By 1868 the Silloth Convalescent Home was open, with each subscriber given tickets to admit only convalescents *of known good character*. During the First World War wounded soldiers, and injured 'munition girls' from Gretna were admitted at 18 shillings a week, Alas, due to 'unsuitable behaviour', no further Gretna girls were taken after 3 months. The Home was requisitioned during the Second World War, with 1,053 casualties admitted in 1945 alone. In 1976 and 1980 the Home ran at a loss but was saved by Silloth Town Council, the staff and its League of Friends. This 1904 picture shows the home and its railway siding off the line to the Armstrong Whitworth Gun Battery.

In the 18th century the remote hamlet of Tarns was a centre for Solway smuggling, with Irish and Scotch Whisk(e)y, wool and tea from the Isle of Man smuggled to Allonby and hidden on Lowsay and Low Tarns Farm nearby. By the 1920's, when Polly and Annie Watson's Tarnside Boathouse and Refreshment Room was open, smuggling was a thing of the past, and trippers could enjoy a relaxing day away from the crowds at Allonby and Silloth. In 2004 this sleepy settlement of a few farms became the venue for the first Solfest annual music, arts and performance festival.

North Lodge, built in 1824 by Darlington born Thomas Richardson (1771-1853) and his Allonby born wife Martha Beeby. A leading member of the Society of Friends, banker, director of the Stockton & Darlington Railway and one of the Middlesborough Six (who financed the building of Middlesborough Docks in 1829), Richardson built the central pavilion as a personal summer residence, with the adjoining four flats, four cottages and two houses let free, with £5 a year pension, to needy Quaker families. The 1851 Census shows three of the properties uninhabited, whilst in the others were: Robert Ostle, a 74 year old mariner and his cousin Rachel Johnston; Mary Grave, a retired Bather woman (who may have worked at Allonby Baths): Mary Brown, a widow companion and her son Thomas; Hannah Beeby, a bookbinder; and John Storey, a retired weaver and his daughter Jane. Today North Lodge is a registered charity home run by Allonby Almshouse Trust.

Allonby Sunshine Home was built as a children's holiday home in 1934 by Margaret Harrison, where on alternate weeks, boys and girls could enjoy a break at the seaside. Accommodation was in dormitories, which the children would tidy before helping prepare breakfast. There would then be trips along the beach or games in the lounge. In 1991 restrictions imposed by the Child and Young Persons Act, and lack of funds, resulted in its closure, and conversion, by Carol and Thomas Thomlinson, to the Sunshine Retirement Home in 1995. In front of the home is Allonby Congregational Chapel built in 1844 with seating for 180 worshippers. The Sunshine Home and the Chapel are now (2007) private houses.

In the 19th century The Square was Allonby's main street and stopping place for the Royal Sailor stagecoach on its daily journey between Carlisle and Whitehaven. A shallow groove cut into the cobbles divided The Square, marking the stage coach road right, and the pitch for Allonby's market traders stalls on the left. The front of Allonby Seawater Baths is just visible on the right beyond the chimneys. Built in 1835 on land donated by Sarah Brockbank Satterthwaite-Clarke, the Baths offered - warm, cold, shower or vapour baths, whilst upstairs, entertainments were held in the elegant ballroom. They closed in the 1880s as tourists deserted Allonby for Silloth.

The Beck, with the entrance to The Square off to the left, and the new main road, passing the Ship Hotel before turning right, over the road bridge. In 1848 the only bridge across The Beck - a stone packhorse style - was in such disrepair that a subscription fund was raised and an iron bridge, engineered by John Hodgson of Carlisle and built by Joseph & William Hodgson, Solway Foundry, Maryport replaced it. However, this bridge was so damaged by a traffic accident in 1905 that it was, in turn, replaced by today's skew-arched bridge.

The Hill and Reading Room, flooded by the sea in winter 1904. This storm looks ferocious, but was minor, compared to the gale force winds that drove the 2,240 ton, four masted barque, *Hougomont*, on to the sands on 25 February 1903. En route from San Francisco to Liverpool via Maryport it was loaded with grain and cases of tinned fruit and salmon. The 30 crewmen were rescued by the Maryport lifeboat, and cargo 'saved' by the brave villagers of Allonby.

The Beck, The Hill and herring boats in the bay. Recent excavations at the seawall of The Hill revealed that the foundations are similar to those at the harbour, but whether The Hill was once Allonby's harbour could not be confirmed. It was once a maritime store for imported wines and spirits shipped in from Liverpool and Whitehaven, and a kippering house. In 1932 the Jackson family opened Allonby Riding School at The Hill, providing pony rides along the beach.

A picturesque view of Allonby of around 1911. Behind the lady is East House with Moss House, built in 1760 by yeoman farmer Thomas Bouch, attached. Behind Moss House is the Reading Room, whilst in the distance can just be seen part of the Solway Hotel and the Grapes Hotel along the terrace. On the left are typical Allonby mariners' cottages with the 1844 built Congregational Chapel.

Looking south from The Beck is Greenbank House on the right, with the Reading Room clock tower behind. Further left is the Baths with its balcony overlooking the Solway and next left, behind the bridge, is Allonby Bazaar. Purchased by Aspatria Industrial Co-operative Society in 1939, the shop later became a *Buywell* store. Across the road is Allonby Hall. Opened in 1905 the Hall front has a clock donated by George Moore (1806-1876), the textile merchant and philanthropist, of Whitehall, Mealsgate.

Service buses going to Silloth from Maryport wait for passengers outside the Ship Hotel. Access to Allonby has always been difficult, with a failed plea made to the omnibus companies in 1864 to reinstate the horse drawn bus from Aspatria Railway Station, and save travellers the Maryport detour. A scheme to construct a coastal rail link from Silloth through Allonby to Netherhall also failed in 1887, when the £30,000 needed could not be raised, and in February 1887 a subscription fund to build a landing stage for sailings to the Isle of Man raised only £24 16/-.

A scattering of holidaymakers on the beach fronting the three storey Solway Hotel. In the 1960s the hotel was a venue for international country and western stars like Boxcar Willie, until gutted by fire. In 1970 a new improved Solway Hotel was opened, but that too was destroyed in 2002, when a roof repairer's blowlamp started another fire. Today it is a residential development. On the right of the photograph are three arched roof cottages named Dundrennan, Lincluden and Burnswark after Scottish villages across the Solway. In the 19th century Allonby Pond, now dried up, was used to moor fishing boats in front of these cottages.

West Green, Allonby in the 1930s with Sydney Thompson's garage and taxi hire business on the corner of Brewery Lane. The golden days of the 1860s, when Allonby's visitors were listed in the *Wigton Advertiser* and could stay in one of Allonby's seven inns, the Globe, Greyhound, New Inn, Ship, Sloop, Sun, or the Swan, or one of 20 boarding houses, were long gone. But, judging by the number of cars parked on West Green was still popular.

West Green with Billy Twentyman's fishing boat (registered at Maryport) ready for launch. In the early 19th century there would have been over 50 boats beached here. Herring was so abundant in 1850s that they sold for one penny each at Whitehaven, but after a decade of good fishing the shoals left the Solway and did not return until 1888 when Allonby's boats and tackle had fallen into decay.

By the 1900s new ships were built with iron hulls, rendering wooden hulled ships obsolete, and many of these, from Maryport, Workington and Whitehaven, were towed to the gently sloping southern shores of Allonby to be broken. Much of the wood was recycled, returning to West Cumbria as pit props, although many good beams were used by locals to rebuild and enlarge their houses.

Wigton Boys Brigade's sixth annual camp, near North House in 1906. The company arrived at Allonby on the Friday evening, 14th July, during a gale, which almost carried away the main tent. The following days were fine, with the boys playing cricket, entertaining visitors and, on the Sunday evening, in accordance with the Brigade's Christian ideals of reverence, discipline and obedience, attending a service at Allonby Parish Church. On Monday morning the troop returned home having managed to consume 14 stones of broken biscuits, 78 bottles of lemonade, fruit, loaves, butter, jam and boiled tongue, all to the value of £27.

The manufacture of Allonby sea salt was the reserve of Holm Cultrum Monastery until the Reformation in 1536, and only in the 1720s did Humphrey Senhouse (1706-1770) landowner and industrialist of Netherhall, Maryport open a coal fired pan at Crosscanonby, near Allonby. It closed in 1736, but the workers' cottages remained occupied until converted into the Seaside Inn in the mid 19th century. In the 1920s it became Anna Maud's tearoom, catering for caravaners and campers. In 1972, when the saltpans became a heritage site, the cottages on the left were removed and the kinch (filter pond) on the right restored.